THIS BOOK BELONGS TO:

____

Made in United States
Troutdale, OR
08/18/2023

12187555R00076